THE GREAT PHILOSOPHERS

Consulting Editors
Ray Monk and Frederic Raphael

BOOKS IN THE GREAT PHILOSOPHERS SERIES

SPINOZA

Roger Scruton

3 1571 00185 9860

ROUTLEDGE
New York

Published in 1999 by
Routledge
29 West 35th Street
New York, NY 10001

First published in 1997 by
Phoenix
A Division of the Orion Publishing Group Ltd.
Orion House
5 Upper Saint Martin's Lane
London WC2H 9EA

10 9 8 7 6 5 4 3 2 1

Library of Congress Cataloging-in-Publication Data

Scruton, Roger.
        Spinoza / Roger Scruton.
          p. cm.—(The great philosophers : 15)
        Includes bibliographical references.
        ISBN 0-415-92390-5 (pbk.)
        1. Spinoza, Benedictus de, 1632–1677. Ethica. 2.
        Ethics. I. Title. II. Series: Great Philosophers
        (Routledge (Firm)) : 15.
B3974.S37 1999
199'.492—dc21   99-22483
                                                          CIP

SPINOZA

LIFE AND CHARACTER

Benedict de Spinoza (1632–77) was born, lived and died in Holland, where his family, who were Jews from Portugal, had come as refugees from the Inquisition. He was brought up in the Jewish faith, but was anathematized for his heretical opinions, which had been acquired during a study of Descartes (1596–1649), the founding father of modern philosophy. Descartes too, although French by birth, had lived for most of his creative life in Holland. Thanks to Descartes and the Cartesians, and thanks to the intellectual freedom enjoyed by the Dutch Republic during the years following its successful revolt against Spain, seventeenth-century Holland was, for a few precious decades, a centre of intellectual life, and the first home of the Enlightenment.

Freedom of thought is more easily lost than won, and with the rise of Calvinism the tolerant regime of the Republic came to an end. In 1670 Spinoza published a *Theologico-Political Treatise*, to which he did not add his name, but which was soon discovered to be his work. This treatise defended secular government, the rule of law and freedom of opinion, and was richly illustrated by biblical examples that did not conceal the author's hostility to the government of priests and pharisees. The *Treatise* was banned, and its author briefly exiled from Amsterdam.

In response to this confrontation with authority, Spinoza

went to live in retirement among dissenting Christians. He retained an interest in politics, and made several hazardous forays into public life. He also began work on a second political treatise that he never finished. But he published nothing further, and his masterpiece, the *Ethics*, which had been circulating among eager students for some years before his death, appeared posthumously, and was promptly banned.

Spinoza led a chaste and studious life, refusing the offer of a professorship at Heidelberg, and developing his thought through correspondence with other scientific and philosophical writers. He had wide-ranging interests, in politics, law, biblical scholarship and painting, as well as in mathematics and physical science. He carried out experiments in optics, and the grinding of lenses for these experiments may have exacerbated the consumption that brought him to an early but peaceful death. He was esteemed by all who knew him, and loved by many. In a letter he wrote:

> So far as in me lies, I value, above all other things out of my control, the joining hands of friendship with men who are lovers of truth. I believe that nothing in the world, of things outside our own control, brings more peace than the possibility of affectionate intercourse with such men; it is just as impossible that the love we bear them can be disturbed ... as that truth once perceived should not be assented to.

That vision of friendship, as bound up with the pursuit of truth, radiates from all Spinoza's writings. Friendship and the pursuit of truth, he believed, contribute to our highest goal – which is *amor intellectualis Dei*, the intellectual love of God. Spinoza's philosophy was an attempt to reconcile this profoundly religious outlook with the scientific view of man.

THE ETHICS

S pinoza wrote in Latin, adopting medieval and Cartesian technicalities, and forging his own style, which was sparse and unadorned, yet solemn and imposing. The occasional aphorisms jump from the page with all the greater force, in that they emerge from arguments presented with mathematical exactitude. There is space here to consider only Spinoza's greatest work, the *Ethics*, whose argument, however, is of such intrinsic relevance to us who live three centuries after its publication that thinking people have as much reason as they had in its author's day to acquaint themselves with its main conceptions.

The *Ethics* is divided into five parts, each of which is set out in the manner of Euclid's geometry, beginning with definitions and axioms, and deducing theorems by abstract proofs. The axioms are supposed to be self-evident, and the theorems valid deductions. If this were so, then the entire philosophy would be not merely true, but necessarily true – in the way that mathematics is necessarily true. The unlikelihood of this should not deter us. Even if the proofs are shaky and the axioms obscure, there is a great intellec-tual treasure to be mined from them, and – judged as a whole and in terms of its underlying agenda – Spinoza's philosophy is nearer to the truth than any other that has addressed the same barely fathomable questions. These questions are just as important for us as they were for Spinoza. The difference is that we are seldom aware of them. Here they are:

1. Why does anything exist?
2. How is the world composed?
3. What are we in the scheme of things?
4. Are we free?
5. How should we live?

Our modern inability to answer these questions accounts for our modern reluctance to confront them, which in turn accounts for our deep disorientation. What is fashionably known as the 'postmodern condition' is really the condition of people who, having given up on their fundamental anxieties, find it easier to conceal them. Such people no longer know what to hope for or how. There is no better therapist for their condition than Spinoza, and no greater advocate of the spiritual life to those who have lost the desire to repossess it.

The five questions that I have listed are philosophical: they cannot be answered by observation and experiment, but only by reasoning. Cosmologists dispute over the 'origins of the Universe', some arguing for a Big Bang, others for a slow condensation. But both theories leave a crucial question unanswered. Even if we conclude that the

Universe began at a certain time from nothing, there is something else that needs to be explained – the 'initial conditions' which then obtained. Something was true of the Universe at time zero – namely, that *this* great event was about to erupt into being, and to generate effects in accordance with laws that were already, at this initial instant, in place. And what is the explanation of *that*?

This is a version of the first question listed above. No scientific theory can answer it. Yet, if it has no answer, nothing really has an explanation. We can describe how the Universe works, but not why it is there. Indeed, the existence of a universe that *works*, a universe that admits of scientific explanations, is an even greater mystery than the existence of random chaos. What immortal hand or eye could frame this fearful symmetry? Or did it just *happen*? And if so, how and why?

Spinoza lived at a time when modern science was beginning to emerge from the hinterground of theological speculation. He was an accomplished scientific thinker, who anticipated many aspects of modern physics and cosmology. But he recognized no absolute divide between science and philosophy. For him, as for Descartes, physics rests upon metaphysics, and a scientist who ignores the fundamental questions does not really understand what he is doing. These fundamental questions cannot be answered by experiment; it is reason and not experience that is our guide to ultimate reality. It is because he thought in this way that Spinoza is described as a rationalist (rather than an empiricist, i.e. one who founds all knowledge on experience). And that is why he adopted the 'geometrical method', since reason knows no other. All the truths of reason are either self-evident or derived from self-evident truths by chains of deductive argument.

The adoption of the geometrical method means that Spinoza's philosophy appears at first sight intolerably austere. It is normal for philosophers to begin from local puzzles, and thereafter to advance by degrees towards an abstract picture of reality. Thus Descartes began by asking himself whether there is anything that he could not doubt, and went on to construct a metaphysical theory that would bring his doubts to an end. Spinoza begins from the point where other thinkers end – from the axioms of an abstract theory. He then *descends* by degrees to the human reality, and to the problems that his theory is supposed to solve. To accomplish this at all is a great achievement; to accomplish it in the manner of Spinoza, so as to provide solutions to the perennial questions, is little short of a miracle.

GOD

The first part of the *Ethics* is devoted to the first two of our questions: why does anything exist? and how is the world composed? Spinoza, like many of his forerunners, was convinced that the Universe lacks an explanation unless there is something which is *cause of itself* – that is, whose nature it is to exist. The explanation of such a thing will be found within itself: it *has* to exist, otherwise it would be in violation of its own definition. This thing that exists necessarily and by its very nature has traditionally been called God, and the first part of the *Ethics* is duly entitled 'On God'. Here, abridging slightly, are the definitions with which it begins:

D1: By cause of itself I understand that whose essence involves existence, *or* that whose nature cannot be conceived except as existing.

D2: That thing is said to be finite in its own kind that can be limited by another of the same nature.

D3: By substance I understand what is in itself and conceived through itself, i.e., that whose concept does not require the concept of another thing, from which it must be formed.

D4: By attribute I understand what the intellect perceives of a substance, as constituting its essence.

D5: By mode I understand the modifications (*affectiones*) of a substance, *or* that which is in another through which it is also conceived.

D6: By God I understand a being absolutely infinite, i.e., a substance consisting of an infinity of attributes, each of which expresses an eternal and infinite essence.

D7: That thing is called free which exists from the necessity of its nature alone, and is determined to act by itself alone. But a thing is called necessary, or rather compelled, which is determined by another to exist and to produce an effect in a certain and determinate manner.

D8: By eternity I understand existence itself, insofar as it is conceived to follow necessarily from the definition of the eternal thing.

Seldom has a great work of philosophy begun so forbiddingly. Already a large part of Spinoza's world-view has been suggested by these eight definitions, and much of the difficulty of the *Ethics* lies in deciphering them.

The first definition is taken from Moses Maimonides, a twelfth-century Jewish thinker who was one of the greatest influences on medieval philosophy. As I remarked above, it seemed to Spinoza that there could be an answer to the riddle of existence only if there were a being whose very nature it is to exist, a being whose existence would be self-explanatory. Such a being must be self-produced, or 'cause of itself'. Hence the definition.

From the same repertoire of theological ideas comes Spinoza's distinction between the finite and the infinite. Finite things, he believes, have limits – whether in space or time or thought. And a thing with limits is limited by something: a larger or greater or more long-lasting thing can always be conceived. Not everything can be compared with (and therefore limited by) everything else. A great elephant is not larger or smaller than a great thought. In general, physical things (bodies) are limited by physical things, and mental things (ideas) by mental things. Hence the expression 'finite in its own kind'.

The third definition introduces the pivotal concept of

Spinoza's philosophy – the concept on which his metaphysical arguments turn. The term 'substance' was one of the technicalities of seventeenth-century philosophy. But each thinker had his own way of using it. According to Spinoza, reality divides into those things that depend upon, or are explained through, other things, and those things that depend upon nothing but themselves. Thus the child derives from its parents, who in turn derive from their parents, who in turn ... The chain of human reproduction is a chain of dependent beings. These are not substances, since to form a true conception of their nature (an explanation of what and why they are) we must conceive them in terms of their causes. 'Substance' is the term Spinoza reserves for the things in which all else inheres or upon which all else depends. Substances are conceived not through their causes, but through themselves. Lesser, dependent, beings are 'modes' of substances. In Definition 5 he calls these lesser things '*affectiones*' – a Latin technicality, meaning, roughly, 'ways in which substances are affected', as a piece of wood is affected by being painted red or a chair by being broken. (If a chair were a substance, then its being broken would be a mode of the chair. But we can already see that, by the definition, nothing so humble and contingent as a chair could be a substance.)

Definition 4 is fraught with controversy. Roughly speaking, here is what Spinoza had in mind. When we understand or explain a substance, it is through knowledge of its essential nature. But there may be more than one way of 'perceiving' this essential nature. Imagine two people looking at a picture painted on a board, one an optician, the other a critic. And suppose you ask them to describe what they see. The optician arranges the picture on two axes, and describes it thus: 'At $x = 4$, $y = 5.2$, there is a patch of chrome yellow; this continues along the horizontal axis until $x = 5.1$, when it changes to Prussian blue.' The critic says: 'It is a man in a yellow coat, with a lowering expression, and steely blue eyes.' You could imagine these descriptions being complete – so complete that they would enable a third party to reconstruct the picture by using them as a set of instructions. But they have nothing whatever in common. One is about colours arranged on a matrix, the other about the scene that we see in them. You cannot switch from one narrative to the other and still make sense: the man is not standing next to a patch of Prussian blue, but next to the shadow of an oak tree. The Prussian blue is not situated next to a coat sleeve, but next to a patch of chrome yellow. In other words, the two descriptions are incommensurate: no fragment of the one can appear in the midst of the other without making nonsense. Yet neither description misses out any feature that is mentioned in the other. This is something like what Spinoza had in mind with his concept of an attribute: a complete account of a substance, which does not rule out other, and incommensurate, accounts of the very same thing.

Spinoza's sixth definition introduces the 'God of the philosophers': the God familiar from countless works of ancient and medieval theology, who is distinguished from all lesser things by the completeness and fullness of his being. He contains 'an infinity of attributes' – in other words, infinitely many accounts can be given of him, each of which conveys an infinite and eternal essence. The idea of the eternal is explained in the final definition, where, in an added clause, Spinoza makes the distinction between eternity and duration. Nothing that is conceived in time can be eternal – at best it endures without limit. True eternity is the eternity of mathematical objects, like numbers, and of the 'eternal truths' that describe them. To be eternal is to lie outside time. All necessary truths are eternal in that sense, like the truths of mathematics. When the existence of something is proved by deductive argument from its definition, then the result is an eternal truth: and God is eternal in just that sense.

The seventh definition tells us that dependent and determined things are not free, in the proper sense of the word. Only self-dependent things – that is, things that accord with the first definition – can be truly free.

Having given us these definitions, Spinoza moves on to the axioms, which are the supposedly self-evident premises of his philosophy. Here they are:

A1: Whatever is, is either in itself or in another.

A2: What cannot be conceived through another, must be conceived through itself.

A3: From a given determinate cause the effect follows necessarily; and conversely, if there is no determinate cause, it is impossible for an effect to follow.

A4: The knowledge of an effect depends on, and involves, the knowledge of its cause.

A5: Things which have nothing in common with one another also cannot be understood through one another, i.e. the conception of the one does not involve the conception of the other.

A6: A true idea must agree with its object.

A7: If a thing can be conceived as not existing, its essence does not involve existence.

The axioms are scarcely less forbidding than the definitions. Spinoza was aware of this, and counselled his readers to follow some of the proofs in order that the meaning and truth of the axioms should be brought gradually home to them. This is not to deny the self-evidence of the axioms, but only the difficulty in achieving the perspective from which their self-evidence will dawn. It is true of geometry and set theory, too, that the axioms are often less clear than the theorems.

The first two axioms nevertheless need elucidating. For Spinoza, 'B is *in* A' is another way of saying that A is the explanation of B. In such a case B must also be 'conceived through' A – which means that no adequate account of the nature of B can fail to mention A (hence Axiom 4). In effect, the first two axioms divide the world into two kinds of thing. The first are those that are dependent on other things (their causes), and which must be conceived through their causes. The second are things that are self-dependent and conceived through themselves. And it should be obvious from the definitions that this is the distinction between modes and substances.

To understand the axioms fully, we need to know what Spinoza wishes to prove. The first part of the *Ethics* consists of 36 propositions and their proofs, together with several extended passages of commentary. They constitute Spinoza's argument for the view that there is one and only one substance, and that this one substance is God, and therefore infinite and eternal. Everything else exists *in* God – that is, it is a mode of God, and as such is dependent upon God. The proof of this remarkable claim follows a pattern familiar from medieval philosophy – the pattern of the 'ontological argument' for God's existence, as Kant was later to call it. Since God is defined as a being with infinite attributes, then nothing exists that could limit or take away his being: in every respect he is without limits. Since non-existence is a privation, a limitation, it cannot be predicated of God. Therefore God's essence involves existence – he is, by Definition 1, 'cause of himself'. However, if we understand this traditional argument for the existence of God correctly, Spinoza reasons, we must see that it does not prove only that God exists, but that God embraces everything – that, outside God, nothing can exist or be conceived. If there is anything other than God, either it is *in* God and dependent upon him, in which case it is not a substance but simply a mode of God, or else (Axiom 1) it is outside God, in which case there is something that God is not – some respect in which God is limited, and therefore finite (Definition 2) – which is impossible (Definition 6). Hence there is in the world only one substance, and this substance is God.

All finite things follow each other in an infinite chain of

cause and effect, and each is determined to be what it is by the cause that produces it. As Spinoza puts it:

Proposition 29: In nature there is nothing contingent, but all things have been determined from the necessity of the divine nature to exist and produce an effect in a certain way.

The one substance is both God and Nature, and can be considered both as the free and self-creating creator (*Natura naturans*) and as the sum of his creation – of those things that are *in* God and conceived through him (*Natura naturata*). In the metaphysical sense, only God is free (see Definition 7). Hence:

Proposition 32: The will cannot be called a free cause, but only a necessary one.

From all this it follows that

Proposition 33: Things could have been produced by God in no other way, and in no other order, than they have been produced.

God, the infinite substance who comprehends everything, is the only free being, in the sense defined in Part 1 of the *Ethics*, since only he fully determines his own nature. Everything else is bound in the chain of causation, whose ultimate ground is God.

It is easy to understand why Spinoza was regarded as such a dangerous heretic. He offered to prove the existence and grandeur of God. But the small print tells us that God is identical with Nature, and that nothing in the world is free.

For the bewildered believer, anxious for a philosophy with which to counter modern science, this is the ultimate sell-out. The inexorable machine of nature is all that there is, and we are helplessly enslaved to it. And the fact that nature is 'cause of itself' – that is, the fact that it exists of *necessity* and could not be other than it is – only adds to the disaster.

GOD'S ATTRIBUTES

Spinoza would have rejected that interpretation of his philosophy. For it overlooks the most important and original of his claims, which is that God has infinitely many attributes, only one of which is studied by physical science. Two of these attributes are thoroughly familiar to us – namely, thought and extension. The term 'extension', taken from the science of Spinoza's day, refers to space and its contents – in other words, to the physical world. Extension is an attribute of God in the sense that a complete theory of the physical world (of extended things) is a theory of all that there is. And thus far modern science would agree with Spinoza. But while physics is, when complete, the truth about the whole, it is not the whole truth. For God can be conceived in other ways. For example, he can be conceived under the attribute of thought. This means that God is essentially a thinking thing, just as he is essentially an extended thing. And by studying the nature of thought, one studies God as he is in himself, advancing towards a complete theory of the world – just as when one studies the nature of extension.

Another way of expressing this point is to say that everything that exists – every mode of the divine substance – can be conceived in two incommensurate ways, as physical or mental. In my own case I have an inkling of what this means – for I know that I have both a mind and a body, the first being composed of ideas (where 'idea' is a general term for all mental entities), the second being composed of particles in space. Spinoza's suggestion is that the relation between mind and body that I perceive in myself is reduplicated through the whole of nature: that everything physical has its mental correlate.

But what *is* the relation between mind and body? This problem has vexed philosophers since ancient times, and had come to a head in Spinoza's day, on account of Descartes' influential argument for the view that I am a mental substance, distinct from my body and only contingently connected with it. By contrast, the second part of the *Ethics* – 'Concerning the Nature and Origin of the Mind' – describes the relation between mind and body as one of identity:

> Part 2, Proposition 21, scholium: The mind and the body are one and the same thing, which is conceived now under the attribute of thought, now under the attribute of extension.

Spinoza thinks that his theory of the attributes enables him to say this, since it implies not only that the one substance can be known in two ways, but that the same two ways of knowing apply also to modes. The mind is a finite mode of the infinite substance conceived as thought; the body is a finite mode of the infinite substance conceived as extension. And another way of saying this (Part 2, Proposition 13) is that the mind is the 'idea of' the body – meaning that the two modes are in fact one and the same reality, conceived in two different ways.

This is a striking claim, with many surprising consequences. For Spinoza, every object in the physical world has its mental counterpart, with which it is identical, in the same way that mind and body are identical in me. The idea of every physical thing already exists – not necessarily in any human mind, but in the mind of God, which comprehends the whole of reality under the attribute of thought. Moreover, there is no interaction between mind and body, despite their identity, for interaction implies cause and effect, and A is cause of B, in Spinoza's thinking, only if B must be conceived *through* A. But nothing conceived under one attribute can be explained in terms of (that is, conceived through) something conceived under another attribute. The world may be one substance, but there is no single theory of its nature, and in particular no way of reducing the mental to the physical.

This theory looks less odd if we forget our own case and look at the minds of others. Suppose I see John waving frantically from the other end of the field. I ask Helen, one of my companions, why John is waving. She replies, 'Electrical impulses from his brain are activating the motor neurones of the arm and producing muscular spasms of a rhythmical kind.' Well yes, that is true. But it is not the answer I was seeking. I turn to Jim and repeat the question. Jim answers: 'He is trying to warn us about a danger somewhere – maybe a bull.' The answer is more pertinent, but no more true.

In this example, both Helen and Jim have given true explanations of what we observe. But one is framed in physical terms, the other in mental terms. One mentions processes in the body, the other conceptions in the mind. As we might put it, the one gives the physical causes of John's action, the other the mental *reasons* for it. And I can relate to the second explanation more readily, since it gives insight into what John *means* – in other words, into his mental states, which have a direct connection with my own intentions. Helen could be the best neurophysiologist in the world; she could give a far more complete explanation of John's waving than any broached by Jim. But the chances are we should both be dead before the explanation ended.

Moreover, the two explanations are incommensurate. You cannot add fragments of Helen's account to fragments of Jim's and achieve a complete account – or any account at all – of John's behaviour. You must take either one route or the other to an explanation of what you see. And that is what Spinoza meant by saying that 'the body cannot determine the mind to think, nor the mind the body to remain in motion or at rest' (*Ethics*, Part 3, Proposition 2).

But what of those finite modes – rocks and stones and trees, tables and chairs, typescripts and coffee cups – that we normally regard as inanimate? Spinoza must say that they are not inanimate at all, and that if I saw them as God sees them then I should be as clearly aware of their mental counterparts as I am aware of my own mind and its ideas. This is not as absurd as it sounds. Consider the following example. When I hear music, I hear a sequence of sounds, distinguished by their pitch, timbre and duration, which are events in the physical world. A physicist can give a thorough description of these sounds as vibrations in the air, and say exactly what they are, in terms of the 'motion and rest' (to use Spinoza's terminology) of things in space. And that is what I hear, when I listen to music. But I also hear these sounds in another way, a way that is not captured by their physical description. I hear a melody, which begins on the first note, rises through an unseen dimension, and falls again. Note responds to note in this melody, as thought responds to thought in consciousness. A musical movement, through musical space, carries on through the sequence, even though no sound moves in the space described by the physicist. A critic, describing the music, is describing the very same objects as the physicist who describes the sounds; and yet he is interpreting them in mental terms, seeing the *intention* that animates the musical line and drives the melody to its logical conclusion. The music is not separate from the sounds. Rather it *is* the sounds, understood through the conceptions that we use when describing the mental life of people. And that, incidentally, is why music is so important to us: it provides a sudden insight into the soul of the world. These rare glimpses into the soul of things enable us to understand what it would be like to see the world as God sees it, and know it not as extension only, but also as thought.

KNOWLEDGE AND ERROR

To understand what Spinoza is trying to say, we must turn to his theory of knowledge. This is contained in the second part of the *Ethics*, Definition 4 of which reads as follows:

> By adequate idea I understand an idea which, in so far as it is considered in itself, without relation to an object, has all the properties, or intrinsic marks of a true idea.

And he adds by way of explanation:

> I say intrinsic in order that I may exclude what is extrinsic, i.e. the agreement of the idea with its object.

This extrinsic mark of truth had been used in Axiom 6 of the first part as a definition of truth. Every idea, understood rightly, is in exact correspondence with its object, since every idea is nothing more than a conception of its object under the attribute of thought. Hence:

> Part 2, Proposition 33: There is nothing positive in ideas, whereby they could be called false.

However, we do not always grasp the relation between an

idea and its object. In sense perception and other forms of 'imagination', our ideas follow each other according to the rhythm of the body, and not according to their intrinsic logic, for 'the human mind perceives no external body as actually existing save through ideas of modifications of its body' (Part 2, Proposition 26). Spinoza gives an example:

> Part 2, Proposition 35, note: ... when we look at the Sun we imagine that it is only some two hundred feet distant from us: which error does not consist in that imagination alone, but in the fact that while we thus imagine it we are ignorant of the cause of this imagination ... we do not imagine the Sun to be near because we are ignorant of the true distance, but because the modification of our body involves the essence of the Sun in so far as the body is affected by it.

My image of the Sun is the mental correlate (the idea) of a physical object. But that object is not the Sun; it is a modification of my body – a brain process, perhaps. By assigning the image to the Sun I fall into error. And this is a paradigm of falsehood, which consists 'in a privation of knowledge, resulting from inadequate or mutilated and confused ideas' (Part 2, Proposition 35).

We can obtain knowledge only through adequate ideas – ideas that guarantee their own truth. The search for such ideas has been the common goal of rationalist philosophers; and it is their common failing that they do not explain quite what an 'intrinsic' mark of truth could be. Spinoza's definition merely substitutes one mysterious term ('adequate') for another ('intrinsic'), and it is only in the course of his argument that we can gain any understanding of his meaning.

However, he does have an example: that of mathematics. The proposition that two straight lines in a plane meet at most only once is an axiom of Euclidean geometry, and seems to be self-evident: its truth is apparent, just as soon as it is understood. And when setting out a mathematical proof, we proceed from proposition to proposition by steps that can be seen to be valid by anyone who understands them. In such a proof we grasp not only the truth of the propositions involved, but also their necessity. And the result is a paradigm of 'adequate' knowledge.

Spinoza argues that God, because he contains the whole of reality, has only adequate ideas, for there is, in God, no 'privation' of knowledge. We, however, are not so lucky. We must strive to amend our thinking, so as to replace our inadequate and confused perceptions (which Spinoza assigns to 'imagination or opinion') with more adequate notions of reality. To return to our example: the Sun cannot be adequately known through modifications of our body, but only through the science which aims to provide an adequate idea of the Sun. This kind of science, proceeding by reasoned reflection from first principles, involves adequate ideas and 'common notions'. A common notion is an idea of some property that is common to everything, and 'those things which are common to all and which are equally in a part and in the whole, can only be conceived adequately' (Part 2, Proposition 38). These notions are common too in another sense: namely, that we all possess them, since we all partake of the common nature that they express. For example, we have an adequate idea of extension, since extension, which runs through all things, runs also through us. And that is why we can recognize the axioms of geometry as self-evident.

Spinoza recognizes another and yet higher level of knowledge, which he calls 'intuition' (*scientia intuitiva*) (Part 2, Proposition 40, Note 2). Intuition is the immediate insight into truth that comes when we grasp a proposition and its proof in a single act of mental attention. An intuition comes to us, he argues, only when we reason from 'an adequate idea of the formal essence of God' – in other words, when we see the exact relation between a thing and the divine substance on which it depends.

For Spinoza, therefore, there are three kinds of understanding: imagination or opinion; the kind of rational science that proceeds through common notions and adequate ideas; and intuition. Understanding of the first kind 'is the only cause of falsity', whereas 'understanding of the second and third kinds is necessarily true' (Part 2, Proposition 41). From our point of view, therefore, the truth of an idea is given in its logical connectedness to the system of adequate ideas, and not merely in its extrinsic correspondence to its object. The advance of knowledge consists in the steady replacement of our confused and inadequate perceptions with adequate ideas until, at the limit, all that we think follows from an adequate idea of the essence of God.

HUMAN NATURE

In the stark metaphysical perspective of Part 1, Spinoza's *Ethics* seems to leave little room for the human being, as a distinct part of God's creation. Whether conceived as mind or as body, I am no more than a finite mode of the divine substance; in what, then, does my individuality consist?

It is only in a problematic sense that God can be spoken of as an individual – as 'one or single' – for an individual is something bounded and finite. What place is there in Spinoza's philosophy for such a thing, or for the distinction that we normally make, between an individual and its properties?

Consider the redness of this book before me. On Spinoza's theory this is a mode of God. Why then should we ascribe the redness to the *book* and not to God, and why are we reluctant to see the book as a *property* of God, in the way that redness is a property of the book? Surely, because we see the book as an independent individual, and not just as a transient state of the divine substance in which it inheres.

There is a sense in which finite modes may be self-dependent, in Spinoza's view, in the way that God is self-dependent. Consider a snowman. This melts away, fragments, is remade and changed and mounts no resistance. There is no real reason why we should regard such a thing as an individual in its own right, rather than as a heap of snow, which in turn is no more than a solid mass of water. By contrast there are finite modes that resist damage, fracture or melting; in some cases, they restore themselves when injured and protect themselves when threatened. They endeavour, as Spinoza puts it, to persist in their own being. This endeavour (*conatus*) is the causal principle in terms of which we explain the persistence and properties of the object that possesses it. The more *conatus* a thing has, therefore, the more it is self-dependent – the more it is 'in' itself.

The obvious examples are organisms. Consider animals: unlike stones they avoid injury, protect themselves when it is threatened, and heal themselves when it is inflicted – unless the injury is so serious as to destroy their *conatus* entirely. For this reason we attribute to animals a self-dependence and an individuality that we rarely accord to insentient things. This is borne out by our way of describing them. A stone is a *lump* of stone, a lake is a *pool* of water, a snowman is a *heap* of snow. But until dead a cat is an individual cat and not a lump of cat, and when dead it is no longer strictly a cat at all, but a lump of catflesh. The individuality and self-dependence of a cat, like those of a man, are part of its *nature*, and to divide a cat in two is to create, not two half-pieces of cat, but two whole pieces of something else. The cat endeavours to persist as *one* thing, and exists just so long as that endeavour is, in Spinoza's idiom, 'granted'. By Definition 2 of Part 2, therefore, the *conatus* of a thing is also its essence:

> Part 2, Definition 2: That pertains to the essence of a thing which, when granted, necessarily involves the

> granting of the thing, and which, when removed,
> necessarily involves the removal of the thing; or that
> without which the thing ... can neither exist nor be
> conceived.

The endeavour of the body is also an endeavour of the mind. Conceived in mental terms, this endeavour is what we mean by will. Sometimes we refer to both body and mind in describing a creature's *conatus*, and then we speak of 'appetite'; sometimes – especially when describing people – we wish to emphasize the element of consciousness that leads them not only to have appetites, but also to be aware of them: then we use the term 'desire' (*cupiditas*) (Part 3, Proposition 9). In every case, however, we are referring to the same reality: the *conatus* that causes an organism to stand apart from its surroundings, in a persistent and active self-dependence.

There is truth in this view of our condition, for if we look at the world with the dispassionate eye of science, we discover very few genuine individuals in it. Under the impact of scientific theory, things break down into the stuff from which they are composed, which further breaks down into molecules and atoms, and finally into energy distributed in space and time – the 'motion and rest' that forms the basis of Spinoza's physics. Only organisms seem to introduce, into our world, some lasting and resistant forms of individuality, and among organisms only those with conscious life and self-understanding seem to behave in God-like ways. To such things we grant proper names, an identity through time, and a self-dependent existence. And the greater their *conatus*, the more God-like they seem, since the activity through which they endeavour to persist in their being presses them to understand and take charge of their condition. Such is our nature, and such is our place in the scheme of things.

Of course, we are apt to mislead ourselves, for 'the human mind, whenever it perceives a thing in the common order of nature, has no adequate knowledge of itself, nor of its body, nor of external bodies, but only a confused and mutilated knowledge thereof' (Part 2, Proposition 29). And from these confused perceptions many of our ordinary beliefs derive, including the belief in free will. Thus:

> Part 2, Proposition 35, note: Men are mistaken in thinking themselves free; and this opinion depends on this alone, that they are conscious of their actions and ignorant of the causes by which they are determined. This, therefore, is their idea of liberty, that they should know no causes of their actions. For when they say that human actions depend on the will, these are words of which they have no idea. For none of them know what is will and how it moves the body; those who boast otherwise and feign dwellings and habitations of the soul, provoke either laughter or disgust.

Strong stuff, and not calculated to endear Spinoza to his pious readers. But an inevitable result, nevertheless, of the theory given in Part 1, and one that presented Spinoza with his supreme challenge as a moralist – how to reconstruct the moral life, in such a way that the popular notion of freedom plays no part in it. And we can already glimpse a part of his brilliant solution. The absolute freedom defined in Part 1, Definition 7, exists in God alone. But there is another, more relative idea of freedom, suggested by the theory of *conatus*. Although only God exists by the necessity of his own nature, and all else depends on him as the all-comprehending cause, finite modes may contain the causes of their activity and persistence to a greater or lesser extent *in* themselves. Even though all causation is to be traced back to the divine essence, the chains that bind us may be either external, operating on us from outside, like the causes that affect a stone, or internal, operating in and through us, like the workings of desire. And the greater the *conatus*, the more inward the chains. By gathering our chains into ourselves, and becoming conscious of their binding force, we also rid ourselves of them, and obtain the only freedom that we can or should desire.

To understand this ingenious idea, we must briefly return to the theory of knowledge.

THE GOD'S-EYE PERSPECTIVE

All ideas exist in God, as modifications of his thinking. Some ideas exist also in the human mind. Spinoza therefore says that our ideas exist in God *in so far as* he constitutes the human mind. Conversely, since God has adequate knowledge of everything, our own ideas are adequate *in so far as* we share in the infinite intellect. This 'in so far as' is a matter of degree: the more adequate my conceptions, the more I reach beyond my finite condition to the divine substance of which I am a mode.

Now it is only in a manner of speaking that we can describe God and his attributes in temporal terms. God is eternal, which means (Part 1, Definition 8) that he is outside time and change. Hence 'things are conceived as actual in two ways – either in so far as they exist in relation to a certain time and place, or in so far as we conceive them as contained in God, and following from the necessity of the divine nature' (Part 5, Proposition 29, note). To pass from the divine to the human perspective is to pass from the timeless to time, and conversely. Although the modifications of God are understood by us as 'enduring' and as succeeding each other in time, this permeation of our knowledge by the concept of time reflects only the inadequacy of our understanding. In so far as we conceive things adequately, we understand them as flowing from God's eternal nature, by a chain of explanation that is logical in form and therefore free from time's dominion in the same way as the truths of mathematics.

Hence 'it is in the nature of reason to perceive things under a certain aspect of eternity' (Part 2, Proposition 44, corollary 2). An adequate conception of the world is a conception 'under the aspect of eternity' (*sub specie aeternitatis*); that is how God sees the world (with which he is identical), and that is how we see it, *in so far as* our minds participate in the vision that is God's.

Spinoza argues that 'the human mind has an adequate

knowledge of the eternal and infinite essence of God' (Part 2, Proposition 47), for what is the *Ethics*, if not a demonstration of our ability to know God as he essentially is, and to know that, apart from God, there is nothing? By achieving adequate knowledge we come to understand what is divine and eternal. On the other hand, we understand our own nature and identity under the aspect of time – *sub specie durationis* – for it is as enduring and finite modes that we enjoy the *conatus* that distinguishes us from the self-sufficient whole of things, and to know *ourselves* as separate individual existences is to be locked in the time-bound conception that leads to confused and partial knowledge. The human condition is one of conflict: reason aspires towards the eternal totality, while the concerns of sensuous existence bind us to what is temporal and partial. The remaining three parts of the *Ethics* set out to prove that our salvation consists in seeing the world *sub specie aeternitatis*, as God sees it, and in gaining thereby freedom from the bondage of time.

ACTION AND PASSION

Part 3 of the *Ethics* deals with the 'origin and nature of the emotions'. Spinoza begins by declaring that he intends to treat this topic with the same geometrical rigour as he had deployed in his discussion of God and the mind:

Such emotions as hatred, anger, envy, etc., considered

in themselves, follow from the same necessity and force of nature as other particular things. And therefore they acknowledge certain causes through which they are understood, and have certain properties as worthy of study as the properties of any other thing the contemplation of which delights us. And so I shall treat of the nature and force of the emotions, and the power of the mind over them, by the same method by which I treated of God and the mind in previous parts, and I shall consider human actions and appetites exactly as if I were dealing with lines, planes and bodies.

The argument sets out from three definitions:

Definition 1: I call that an adequate cause whose effect can be clearly and distinctly perceived through it. I call that one inadequate or partial whose effect cannot be understood through itself alone.

Definition 2: I say that we act when something happens in us or outside us of which we are the adequate cause … On the other hand I say we are passive when something takes place in us … of which we are only the partial cause.

Definition 3. By emotion (*affectus*) I understand the modifications of the body by which the power of action of the body is increased or diminished, aided or restrained, and at the same time the ideas of these modifications.

The first definition brings together two key concepts: cause and adequate idea. For Spinoza, causation is another name for explanation; the relation between cause and effect is therefore an *intellectual* relation, like the relation between premise and conclusion in a mathematical proof. The perfect (adequate) explanation is also a deduction. In such an explanation, knowledge of the effect follows from knowledge of the cause.

Spinoza then defines action and passion: I am active in respect of those things that are fully explained through my own nature, passive in relation to those that must be explained through external causes. Activity and passivity, so defined, are matters of degree.

The definition of emotion reflects Spinoza's theory of the relation between mind and body. An emotion is a bodily condition, and at the same time the idea of that condition. It is what happens in us, when our activity is increased or diminished – activity being both mental and physical.

From these beginnings, Spinoza sets out his strange and forbidding theory of the moral life – a theory that also contains some of the wisest maxims that have ever issued from the pen of a philosopher. He first argues that the mind is active in so far as it has adequate ideas, passive in so far as it has inadequate ideas (Part 3, Proposition 1). The distinction between doing things and suffering things is a distinction of degree, and, since only God is the full and originating cause of anything, only he acts without being acted upon. But we can become more God-like by ascending the ladder of knowledge, replacing our confused perceptions with the adequate ideas that bring understanding and power.

Spinoza's conception of mental activity corresponds only distantly to our ordinary idea of will and agency – ideas that he dismisses in any case as confused. But consider this example: I am pushed from behind and fall on the eggs that I am carrying, so breaking them. Here we should say, not that I broke the eggs, but that the eggs were broken, as a result of someone pushing me. The effect proceeded from an external cause. If, however, I decide to cast the eggs to the ground, it is I who am the cause of their destruction. And the more deliberate my decision, the more responsible I am. Reasoning, which gives me a clear conception of what I do, makes *me* the cause of it. And that, roughly, is what Spinoza means by action – an effect that follows from an idea that clearly conceives it.

Of course, ideas do not, in Spinoza's thinking, have physical effects. But to every idea in the mind there corresponds a modification of the body. When a physical effect is described as an action, we mean that its physical cause is the correlate of a more or less adequate idea. And the more adequate the idea, the more is the cause internal to the agent – the more does it belong to the *conatus* that defines him. In a very real sense, therefore, adequacy of ideas means power. The rational person is the one who strives always to increase his power, to change passion to action, and to secure for himself the joy, independence and serenity that are the true marks of freedom. To achieve this condition, however, is to amend our emotions – to master that in our nature which otherwise might master us.

THE EMOTIONS

Emotions result from the increase or decrease of power, and power is perfection. Joy is the passion with which we proceed to a higher perfection, sadness the passion with which we sink to a lower (Part 3, Proposition 11). Our essence is the striving (*conatus*) with which we endeavour to persist in our own being. When this striving is related only to the mind, it is called will; when referred to both mind and body, it is called appetite. Desire is appetite together with the consciousness thereof (Part 3, Proposition 9). So desire is the very essence of man. As our desires are fulfilled or frustrated, so we experience joy or sadness. But since the objects of desire are various, so too are the occasions of suffering and joy. In his account of the emotions, Spinoza tries to give a systematic theory of human desires, to show how the emotions arise from them, and to warn us against the passions that will undermine our power. This enterprise occupies him in Part 3, where he describes the various emotions, and in Part 4 – 'on human servitude, or the power of the emotions' – in which he explores the paths that we may take to liberation.

For Spinoza, mind and body move in parallel. Every change in bodily power is also a change in mental power and vice versa.

Part 3, Proposition 11: The idea of any thing that increases or diminishes, aids or restrains, our body's power of acting, increases or diminishes, aids or restrains, our mind's power of thinking.

Thus bodily injury, which reduces our body's power of acting, has its mental parallel in pain, which reduces our power of thinking. Our emotional life stems from this close complicity of mind and body. The mind strives to imagine those things that enhance the body's power, and to blot out the images of adversity and failure (Part 3, Propositions 12 and 13). But the influence is reciprocal, and the more inadequate our understanding, the more the body and the external causes that afflict it exert their control. We become passive when our ideas follow bodily processes of which we have only a partial understanding, and this passivity is what we mean by human servitude.

Underlying Spinoza's approach are two powerful insights into the emotional life. The first is that emotions derive from our nature as embodied creatures, propelled by forces that we do not wholly understand. The second is that emotion is nevertheless a form of thought, in which a greater or lesser activity of the mind is expressed. Emotional corruption is also intellectual corruption, and the person who is led by his passions is one who has a defective knowledge of the world.

Because emotions are forms of thought, they may be changed through reasoning. We can argue with the jealous person, and show that his jealousy is mistaken, exaggerated or misplaced. Moreover, we can study emotions in their mental aspect, and discover which of them are good for us, and which of them bad. In this context 'good' means 'useful' (Part 4, Definition 1), and those emotions are useful to us which enable us to flourish according to our nature – in other words, to increase our power. It is obvious, therefore, that all passions, in so far as they are passions, should be transcended, by obtaining a more adequate idea of their object and of its linkage to oneself. But some emotions resist this act of transcendence – hatred, for example, which ceases to be hatred just as soon as it is fully understood (Part 4, Proposition 46). The same is true of all those emotions that involve a downward slope in power and perfection – all those that are forms of sadness, such as envy, jealousy, lust, rage and fear. Emotions that are forms of joy, by contrast, involve a transition from a more passive to a more active frame of mind, and therefore are in agreement with reason: love is an example. (Spinoza defines love, in the appendix to Part 3, as 'joy accompanied by the idea of an external cause'.) Hence love does not demand the same emendation as hatred. Nevertheless, 'love and desire can be excessive' (Part 4, Proposition 44), since the physical correlate of joy is pleasure; love can become fixated on this pleasure, and thereby deprive the body of its versatility and power (Part 4, Proposition 43). Even in their most powerful forms, however, the passions have no power over us that is greater than the power of reason, since 'to every action to which we are compelled by an emotion which is a passion, we can be determined by reason, without such an emotion' (Part 4, Proposition 59). In such ways Spinoza contrives to justify his preferred way of life, in which a kind of godly tranquillity overcomes the turbulence of passion, as reason brings the disordered material of emotion into line with its more adequate conceptions.

The details of Spinoza's 'geometry of the passions' lie beyond our scope. But the reader will ask, nevertheless, why any of it should be accepted. From a sceptical standpoint, Spinoza's adroit definitions and slippery proofs might seem to move too easily to a foregone conclusion, without compelling us to accept it. Ever since Plato, philosophers have advocated the ascent from the world of human passion to the serene realm of reason; yet their morality comes too pat; seems too clearly designed to justify their chosen lifestyle, derives too obviously from their remoteness from the life that they despise. And why is Spinoza any more persuasive than the rest of them? Thus Nietzsche wrote of

> the hocus-pocus in mathematical form, by means of which Spinoza has as it were clad his philosophy in mail and mask – in fact, the 'love of *his* wisdom', to translate the term fairly and squarely – in order thereby to strike terror at once into the heart of the assailant who should dare to cast a glance on that invincible maiden, that Pallas Athene ...

And he added: 'how much of personal timidity and vulnerability does this mask of a sickly recluse betray!' (*Beyond Good and Evil*, 1, 5).

Such criticism overlooks what is most striking and original in Spinoza's vision. He does not advocate a victory of mind over body, nor does he defend the ascetic way of life.

37

Spinoza believes that mind and body are identical, and that the health of the one is inextricably bound up with the health of the other. We are essentially embodied, desiring, striving creatures. Yet we are buffeted and bruised by things outside us, and locked with them into the system of cause and effect. In such circumstances there is only one true wisdom, which is to increase our power, and to ensure that, in so far as it is possible, the things that happen to us are also produced by us.

Philosophy consists in thought. And if Spinoza is right, thought cannot directly change the body, but only the mind. At the same time, by improving the mind, we improve the body. It is a necessary truth that the philosopher's advice must be addressed to the mind of the reader, with a view to enhancing his understanding. A philosopher is a thinker, not a gymnast. Only if the enhancement of understanding is an increase in power can the philosopher's advice be useful. If we see things rightly, however, the ascent of the ladder of reason, from confused perceptions to adequate ideas, can *only* be an increase in the power of the mind. In the mental sphere, this is what power consists in – namely, completeness of knowledge. The advice that Spinoza gives, therefore, is the only advice that ever could be given by a philosopher. And the burden of his metaphysics is to show that the advice is justified.

THE FREE MAN

Spinoza tells us that we are essentially desiring, acting creatures; but he also argues that 'a desire that arises from reason cannot be excessive' (Part 4, Proposition 61). So long as we conduct our lives by the rule of reason, therefore, we shall be living in accordance with our true nature, and achieving fulfilment.

Now it is in the nature of reason to see the world *sub specie aeternitatis* – that is, without reference to time. Reason therefore makes no distinction between past, present and future, and is as much and as little affected by present things as by things in the future or the past (Part 4, Proposition 62.) Only if we see the world *sub specie durationis* are we tempted to lose ourselves in the pursuit of present temptation. But we can have only inadequate ideas of duration and enduring things, so that, in giving way to this 'life in the present moment', we lose sight of what we are doing, and become the passive instruments of external causes.

The one who lives by the dictates of reason is the 'free man' – the person who is active rather than passive in all that involves him. The illusory idea of free will stems from inadequate and confused perceptions; rightly understood, however, freedom is not the release from necessity but the *consciousness* of necessity that comes when we see the world *sub specie aeternitatis* and ourselves as bound by its immutable laws. The free man, in Spinoza's encomium, is a lofty but cheerful character, with no traces of Calvinist gloom. He 'thinks of nothing less than of death, and his wisdom is a meditation on life, not on death' (Part 4, Proposition 67). He steadfastly pursues the good and avoids evil, is robust in overcoming dangers, and also in avoiding them, and is scrupulously honest (Part 4, Proposition 72). But he is not solitary, since 'a man who is guided by reason is more free in a state where he lives according to common decision than in solitude where he obeys himself alone' (Part 4, Proposition 73). This thought is one that Spinoza developed in more detail in his political writings. Although he had a sceptical view of the common people, and their ability to live by the dictates of reason, he nevertheless recognized the need for their company. It is true that 'a free man who lives among the ignorant strives, as far as he can, to avoid their favours' (Part 4, Proposition 70); but, as Spinoza adds, 'though men may be ignorant, they are still men, who in situations of need can bring human aid – and there is no better aid to be had' (ibid.). And although 'only free men are very grateful to one another' (Part 4, Proposition 71), free men are as much in need of political order as the ignorant, and must therefore live according to the law imposed upon them by the 'common decision'.

In his *Political Treatise*, Spinoza argues that 'the true aim of government is liberty'. By 'liberty' he means neither free will (which is metaphysically impossible) nor the kind of freedom discussed in Part 4 of the *Ethics*. He means the ability of people to pursue their projects in peace, and to entertain the opinions and ambitions that reason dictates to them, without interference from the state. His concern for political freedom arose from his suspicion of ordinary people, who are never pleased by beliefs, habits and ambitions other than their own. The art of good government is to enable such people to accept a regime in which the free man may live as his conscience directs. Spinoza is sometimes hailed as a defender of democracy. It would be better to see him as a defender of the liberal constitution, who sought to impart to the offices of government the wisdom that is usually absent from the heads of those who sit in them. Politics, for Spinoza, is the art of survival in the midst of ignorance.

Politics intrudes into the *Ethics* only glancingly. Nevertheless, it is very much in Spinoza's mind when, at the end of Part 4, he summarizes his moral conclusions in a long appendix. The following extracts will convey some of the flavour of this remarkable and uncompromising homily:

> In life ... it is especially useful to perfect, in so far as we can, our intellect or reason, and this is man's highest happiness or blessedness – for blessedness is nothing but the contentment of mind that stems from the intuitive knowledge of God.

> No life ... is rational without understanding, and things are good only in so far as they help man to enjoy the life of the mind ... But those things which prevent man from perfecting his reason and enjoying a rational life – those only we call evil.

> It is, judged from the absolute perspective, permissible

for everyone to do, by the highest right of nature, whatever he judges will be of advantage to him.

Nothing is more useful to man in preserving his being and enjoying a rational life than a man who is guided by reason.

Minds ... are conquered not by arms, but by love and generosity.

It is especially useful to men to form associations, to bind themselves by those bonds most apt to make one people of them, and absolutely to do those things which serve to strengthen friendship.

But skill and vigilance are required for this. For men vary – there being few who live according to the rule of reason – and generally they are envious and more prone to vengeance than to compassion. So it requires a singular power of mind to deal with each according to his own understanding, and to contain oneself and refrain from imitating the emotions of those with whom one has to deal.

Although men are as a rule governed in everything by lust, yet from their common society many more advantages than disadvantages flow. Hence it is preferable to bear their wrongs with equanimity, and to be zealous for those things which produce harmony and friendship.

A purely sensual love ... and absolutely all love that has a cause other than freedom of mind, easily passes into hate – unless (which is worse) it is a kind of madness.

42

In despondency there is a false appearance of morality and religion. And though despondency is the opposite of pride, yet the despondent man is very near to the proud man.

Because ... shame is a species of sadness, it does not belong to the exercise of reason.

Apart from men we know no particular thing in nature whose mind we can enjoy, and which we can join to ourselves in friendship ... And so whatever there is in nature apart from men, the principle of seeking our own advantage does not demand that we preserve it.

Since those things are good which assist the parts of the body to perform their function, and joy consists in the fact that man's power ... is aided or increased, all things that bring joy are good.

Superstition, on the other hand, seems to maintain that the good is what brings sadness, and the evil what brings joy.

Human power is very limited, and infinitely surpassed by the power of external causes. So we do not have an absolute power to adapt things outside us to our use. Nevertheless, we shall bear with equanimity whatever happens to us contrary to our advantage, provided we are conscious that we have done what we ought, that the power we possess could not have been extended to avoid those things, and that we are part of the whole of nature, whose order we follow. If we understand this clearly and distinctly then that part of us which is

43

defined by the understanding – the better part of us – will be entirely satisfied, and will strive to persevere in its satisfaction. For insofar as we understand, we can want nothing except what is necessary, nor absolutely be satisfied with anything except what is true. Hence, in so far as we understand these things rightly, the striving of the better part of us agrees with the order of the whole of nature.

THE HIGHER LIFE

The fifth part of the *Ethics*, subtitled 'On the Power of the Intellect, or on Human Freedom', is more or less entirely given over to a discussion of God, and the relation between God and man. Spinoza has already argued against the popular conception of freedom, according to which we choose always among open possibilities. The very idea of possibility stems from ignorance.

> I call ... individual things possible in so far as, while we regard the causes by which they must be produced, we do not know whether they are determined to produce them. (Part 4, Definition 4)

The more we know of the causality of our actions, the less room we have for ideas of possibility and contingency. However, the knowledge of causality does not cancel the belief in freedom, but vindicates it. It is the *illusory* idea of

44

freedom, arising from imagination, that creates our bond-age, for we believe in the contingency of things only in so far as our mind is passive. The more we see things as necessary (through the medium of adequate ideas), the more we increase our power over them, and so the more we are free (Part 5, Proposition 6). As we have seen, therefore, the free man is conscious of the necessities that compel him.

Such a person understands himself and his emotions, and also loves God, 'and the more so the more he understands himself and his emotions' (Part 5, Proposition 15). This love, which stems necessarily from the pursuit of knowledge, is an intellectual love (*amor intellectualis Dei*). That is to say, the mind is wholly active in loving God, and hence rejoices constantly, but without passion, in the object of its contemplation. God himself can experience neither passion, nor joy nor sorrow (Part 5, Proposition 17), and is therefore free from emotion, as we normally under-stand it. He neither loves the good nor hates the wicked: indeed he loves and hates no one (Part 5, Proposition 17, corollary). Hence, 'he who loves God cannot endeavour to bring it about that God should love him in return' (Part 5, Proposition 19). Love towards God is wholly disinterested, and 'cannot be polluted by an emotion either of envy or jealousy, but is cherished the more, the more we imagine men to be bound to God by this bond of love' (Part 5, Proposition 20). Indeed, man's intellectual love of God 'is the very love of God with which God loves himself' (Part 5, Proposition 36). In loving God we participate more fully in the divine intellect, and in the impersonal, universal love that reigns there, for although God cannot reciprocate our love, he nevertheless loves men, in so far as he loves himself in and through men. This eternal love constitutes our 'salvation, blessedness or liberty'.

During the course of his discussion of man's blessedness, Spinoza gives a singular proof of our immortality – or rather, of the proposition that 'the human mind cannot be absolutely destroyed with the human body, but something of it remains which is eternal' (Part 5, Proposition 23). The obscure proof of this depends upon Spinoza's view that, through adequate ideas, the mind comes to see the world *sub specie aeternitatis*, and therefore without reference to time. The essence of the mind consists in the capacity for adequate ideas. (Essence = *conatus* = activity = adequacy.) The instantiation of this essence in time (in the world of duration) cannot be explained by adequate ideas, since they contain no temporal reference. Such ideas are given 'duration' only through their attachment to the mortal body, and not intrinsically:

> Our mind therefore can be said to endure, and its existence can be defined by a certain time, only in so far as it involves the actual existence of the body, and thus far only does it have the power to determine the existence of things by time, and to conceive them under the aspect of duration. (Part 5, Proposition 23, scholium)

We should not think of eternity as endless duration – since that is to confuse eternity with time. The eternity that we achieve through our thinking is like an escape from time to another dimension. The eternal part of us does not endure after death, but only because it does not endure in life. It comprises a vision, a point of view, a perspective outside time and change, in which we are one with God and redeemed by our knowledge of him. This blessed state is 'not the reward of virtue, but virtue itself; nor do we enjoy it because we restrain our lusts; on the contrary, because we enjoy it, we are able to restrain them' (Part 5, Proposition 42).

That – the last proposition of the *Ethics* – is Spinoza's answer to the religions of the ignorant, whose view of the after-life, as reward or punishment for behaviour here below, is an opinion 'so absurd as to be hardly worth mentioning' (Part 5, Proposition 41). Nevertheless the truth about our relation to God is both difficult and forbidding, and it is not surprising if ignorant people are unable to discover it. Hence, just as virtue is its own reward, so ignorance is its own punishment:

> not only is the ignorant man troubled in many ways by external causes, and unable ever to possess true peace of mind, but he also lives as if he knew neither himself, nor God, nor things; and as soon as he ceases to be acted upon, he ceases to be. On the other hand, the wise man, in so far as he is considered as such, is hardly troubled in spirit, but being, by a certain eternal necessity, conscious of himself, and of God, and of things, he never ceases to be, but always possesses true peace of mind.

> If the way I have shown to lead to these things now seems very hard, still it can be found. And of course, what is found so rarely must be hard. For if salvation were at hand, and could be found without great effort, how could nearly everyone neglect it? But all things excellent are as difficult as they are rare.

With those famous words Spinoza concludes his argument, bequeathing to posterity what is perhaps the most enigmatic book of philosophy that has ever been written.

CONCLUSION

In this brief summary, I have paid scant attention to the detail of Spinoza's proofs. Suffice it to say that their validity has ceaselessly been called in question by Spinoza's critics, who have accused him of bending the argument towards the conclusion desired. Still, how many philosophers are innocent of that failing? It would be more just to see Spinoza's quasi-geometrical proofs as bearing witness to his great elasticity and vigour of mind, and to his unparalleled gift for seeing far-reaching connections.

With the bare minimum of concepts, most of them taken or adapted from medieval and Cartesian philosophy, Spinoza undertook what has rarely been attempted, and never so boldly or arrogantly achieved: he gave a description in outline of all that there is, and a guide in detail as to how to live with it.

This is where we should take a step back from the *Ethics*, and ask ourselves what it means for *us* who think with other concepts, and in a more sceptical age. Here, I believe, is what Spinoza has to say to us:

The physical world is all that there is, and it is a system bound by laws that relate every part of it to every part. These laws can explain what we observe only if the system as a whole has an explanation – only if there is an answer to the question: why is there anything at all? But the cause of the world cannot exist outside it, for then the link between the world and its cause would be unintelligible. Nor can the cause be inside the world, for it is either a part of the world, and therefore unable to explain it, or the whole of the world, in which case the world is self-explanatory.

In other words, the world must be 'cause of itself': its existence must follow from its nature. But when we explain the world in this way, we are not engaged in ordinary science. The scientist explains one thing in terms of another, only by assuming a relation in time between them. When deducing the existence of the world, however, we are dealing with relations of logic, which are outside time and change.

We can easily see that this must be so. In the nature of the case, no scientific theory could explain why the Universe came into existence just when it did, for before that time there was nothing, and therefore nothing in terms of which this 'coming into existence' could be explained. Science, which links events in temporal chains, comes unstuck when there is no *previous* event to the one that needs explaining. Only if we step outside the temporal sphere, and see the world 'under a certain aspect of eternity' can we hope to solve the mystery of its origins.

There are cosmological theories that try to avoid this difficulty, by espousing the idea that there is no first moment – that time is a closed system, like a circle, which constantly returns to any given moment. If that is so, then no moment has any greater claim to be the beginning than any other. But even if we can make sense of this (and it is surely not obvious that we can), it leaves the crucial question unanswered: the question why such a temporal order should exist at all.

This mystery is solved only if the total system is such that it *must* exist, for only then could we have a logical argument for its existence, an argument that deduces the existence of the system without reference to time. It must exist, Spinoza argues, because there is nothing that could negate it. The total system of the world is self-dependent, and conceived through itself. Nothing that we encounter can take its existence away, since everything we encounter is a part of it, and explained through it.

The self-dependent cause of all things is what people have called God, and if this description applies to the total system of physical reality, then that is what God is. But it is not *all* that he is, for a crucial feature of our world is left out of physics: the feature of mind or consciousness. When the physicist lays down the laws of motion of the Universe, he deals in terms of space, time, matter and energy (or 'motion and rest', as Spinoza called it). And he reduces the world without remainder to those all-comprehending variables. Where you and I find thought and feeling, he finds only organisms with central nervous systems; where you and I find intention, desire and rational action, he finds only complex patterns of stimulus and response, mediated by some information-processing software. Yet we need only look into ourselves to discover that this is not all there is – that the crucial fact of consciousness, that strange transparency which veneers the world, has been left out of the physicist's account, for the simple reason that the account is, as it must be, complete without it. Everything physical has been included in his inventory, and nothing else remains.

But there is another aspect to things, and we know it from our own experience. All that the physicist describes as spatial and material can be redescribed as mental – not just you and me, but the entire world. If it were only you and I who could be described in mental terms, then mind would be a mystery, for there could be no *physical* explanation of what distinguishes us from the rest of nature (the mind being unmentionable in physics), and no *mental* explanation either. If the world contains anything mental at all, then it is mental through and through. And have we not felt from time to time that this might be so, felt, with Wordsworth,

> the sentiment of Being spread
> O'er all that moves and all that seemeth still;
> O'er all that, lost beyond the reach of thought
> And human knowledge, to the human eye
> Invisible, yet liveth to the heart;
> O'er all that leaps and runs, and shouts and sings,
> Or beats the gladsome air; o'er all that glides
> Beneath the wave, yea, in the wave itself,
> And mighty depth of waters . . . ?
>
> (*The Prelude*, Book 1, 401–9)

And when, a few lines later, Wordsworth describes himself as 'With God and Nature communing', we need only change 'and' to 'or' for the thought to be Spinoza's.

But if we see the world in this way – and there is no other vision that is both true to science, and true to our knowledge of ourselves – then we cannot hope to be released from natural laws, or to stand apart from the chain of causality. If we are free, then it must be in another and more elevated sense than that proclaimed in the old religions. Freedom can reside only in a *point of view*, a way of looking upon the system of necessity. And are we not all of us, in our thinking moments, familiar with what this means? Surely this is the one freedom that we may attain to: not to be released from physical reality, but to *understand* reality and ourselves as part of it, and so be reconciled to what we are. This work of reconciliation is the true religion, and it is what we owe to ourselves, and to the God from whom our being flows.

If this is so, however, Spinoza is right in thinking that we must strive to see the world under the aspect of eternity. There is no other release from the chain of causality than the kind of thinking that looks beyond causality, to the meaning and pattern of the whole. And when we discover this pattern, things change for us, as a landscape changes when the painter elicits its form, or sounds change when they are combined together as music. A kind of personality shines then through the scheme of things. We come face to face with God, in the very fact of his creation.

If religion is to be reconciled with science, it can be only in Spinoza's way. Spinoza is right in believing that God's majesty is diminished by the idea that things might have been otherwise. The belief in miracles does no credit to God, for what need has God to intervene in events that he originates? The laws of the Universe must be universally binding if we are to understand them, and the intelligibility of the Universe is the premise from which all science and all religion begin.

Nor should we disparage Spinoza's moral vision, remote though it may seem in our age of sensuous indulgence. Spinoza is right to believe that truth is our only standard, and that to live by any other is to surrender to circumstance. There is implanted in every rational being the capacity to distinguish the true from the false, to weigh evidence, and to confront our world without illusions. In this capacity our dignity resides, and in committing ourselves to truth we stand back from our immediate concerns and see the world as it should be seen – under the aspect of eternity. Truth cannot be fashionable, even if it so often offends. To take truth as our guide is to ponder time and all its minions with a sceptical disfavour.

Our age is more dominated by scientific theory than was Spinoza's; but only a fond illusion persuades us that it is more guided by the truth. We have seen superstition triumph on a scale that would have startled Spinoza, and which has been possible only because superstition has cloaked itself in the mantle of science. If the heresies of our day are, like Nazism and communism, the declared enemies of religion, this merely confirms, for the student of Spinoza, their superstitious character, and confirms, too, Spinoza's insight that scientific objectivity and divine worship are the forms of intellectual freedom. Spinoza, like Pascal, saw that the new science must inevitably 'disenchant' the world. By following truth as our standard, we chase from their ancient abodes the miraculous, the sacred and the saintly. The danger, however, is not that we follow this standard – for we have no other – but that we follow it only so far as to lose our faith, and not so far as to regain it. We rid the world of useful superstitions, without seeing it as a whole. Oppressed by its meaninglessness, we succumb then to new and less useful illusions – superstitions born of disenchantment, which are all the more dangerous for taking man, rather than God, as their object.

The remedy, Spinoza reminds us, is not to retreat into the pre-scientific world-view, but to go further along the path of disenchantment; losing both the old superstitions and the new, we discover at last a meaning in truth itself. By the very thinking that disenchants the world we come to a new enchantment, recognizing God in everything, and loving his works in the very act of knowing them.